Oak Ayling

With Love from the Curator

Indigo Dreams Publishing

First Edition: With Love from the Curator
First published in Great Britain in 2021 by:
Indigo Dreams Publishing
24, Forest Houses
Cookworthy Moor
Halwill
Beaworthy
Devon
EX21 5UU
www.indigodreams.co.uk

Oak Ayling has asserted her right under the Copyright, Designs and Patents Act 1988 to be identified as the author of this work.
© Oak Ayling 2021

ISBN 978-1-912876-45-7

British Library Cataloguing in Publication Data. A CIP record for this book can be obtained from the British Library.

This book is sold subject to the condition that it shall not, by way of trade or otherwise, be lent, re-sold, hired out, or otherwise circulated without the author's and publisher's prior consent in any form of binding or cover other than that in which it is published and without a similar condition including this condition being imposed on the subsequent purchaser.

Designed and typeset in Palatino Linotype by Indigo Dreams.
Cover design from artwork by Jane Burn.
Printed and bound in Great Britain by 4edge Ltd.

Papers used by Indigo Dreams are recyclable products made from wood grown in sustainable forests following the guidance of the Forest Stewardship Council.

To the Shark on the corner of always and never.

Acknowledgements

Grateful acknowledgement is made to the following Museums and their staff: the London Natural History Museum and its employees, especially those working as a part of the Dino-Snores project; the Serpukhov Museum of History and Art, especially their faithful Door Cat Maray; Manchester Museum for their fantastic Fossils exhibit, from which the bullet points in *Extinction* were paraphrased; the Smithsonian National Museum of Natural History and their phenomenal virtual tour galleries: the Onomichi City Museum of Art and their associates Ken-chan and Go-chan; the Harvard Museum of Natural History, Christina Davis and Jen Bervin whose "This Object" exhibit reimagining the 'object temporarily removed' signs served as inspiration for *The Resurrection of Something Lost (2019) Somewhere in Harvard*: the Chichibu Chinsekikan and their many curious Jinmenseki; the Mori Building Digital Art Museum from teamLab Borderless, an absolutely stunning creation. And to the following individuals whose work also served to inspire this book: Richard Fortey for his marvellous book *Dry Store Room No.1: the secret life of the natural history museum* – which has probably influenced this collection more than I even realise; Mister Finch, the incredible artist referenced in *Natural History* and *Christmas Display*; Anthony D'Amato for just being an adult at the Dinosaur Museum in Colorado; David Koepp and Michael Crichton – yes I did reference Jurassic Park in this book, you'll find that in *Extinction*: A.A. Milne, for the inclusion of some famous stuffed animals in here too.

    Great thanks also must be given to my best friend Emilie Gill, especially for sleeping under a whale with me, and to my best friend Stephanie Andrew for her never-ending support and encouragement, without the two of you I could well have ended up an Island. I'd also like to give thanks to my family for their daily support and love, to my Dog, Patrick, whose company is preferable at times to most people and to my warm-hearted publishers and editors Dawn Bauling and Ronnie Goodyer, thank you for giving a home to this book and to its novice composer.

CONTENTS

Understanding Extinction 7

Reservations at the London Natural History Museum 8

Unless We Make It Ours 9

The Closing of the Exhibit 10

Emu, Petrified 11

Closet Museum 12

Museum of Flat-pack Furniture 13

The Humours, the Lancet & the Leeches 14

Museum of Broken Hands 15

After Hours 16

Natural History 17

Higamus Hogamus 18

Christmas Display 19

Extinction 20

Heritage 21

The Museum of Flightless Things 22

The Smithsonian in Bed 23

Two Cats from Onomichi 25

The Resurrection of Something Lost 26

Chinsekikan 27

Digital Art Museum 28

Gift Shop 29

A for Mammals, B for Birds, C for Reptiles & so on 30

Understanding Extinction

Scientists study specimens of extinct birds in museums, ask them about their childhoods, where they once lived, what they had expected from marriage, if there's anything they wished they'd done differently regarding how they lived their lives, & then draw from their confessions parables explaining why they became extinct. This is important as it can be used to assist in understanding how rare species can be protected effectively.

A great many flightless birds have become extinct, the Moa for example, hunted into inexistence. Today Common Swifts may spend almost a year without landing; yet, flight has a significant biological cost. Chiefly the price being an inability to carry growing offspring about in the body. There is no bird which is viviparous (bringing forth living young).

Specimens of extinct animals & plants are also important as they are the only certain evidence that a species once existed. For their sake & that of future generations, they are celebrated & preserved in museums.

Reservations at the London Natural History Museum

Marble that looks like a ruined city
You stare hard & bite your tongue
But I think it too
We were that city once.
The frozen animals watch
Us like oncoming cars
You hold my hand tighter
The darkened halls forget to breathe
Shuddering with desire to go deeper
No place was more haunting than this.
A creature I once thought peaceful
Brandishes its jagged thumb
Rearing up to make a mockery of your giant frame
You lead me through the back doors
& shadows
To rooms beyond the second floor
Drawers & drawers of papers
The wings of magpies
Sharks' teeth & palm sized pups
Still born
You look at me
& mouth the word
"Complete"
I rub tears against your cheek
Chase them down
To where the geodes make their stars behind glass
You sit there & hold me
Between your knees & arms
Whisper softly about every creature's history but our own.

Unless We Make It Ours

You fill up all my mother's china cabinets with ammonites
Say, Darling, where do you want the celestial planetarium?
It's Thursday by the time we've sorted butterflies into drawers
Not all lives are unboxed like this; that I know
Home was a word so blurry when we were young
      You say it's not home unless we make it ours
Unless we string up these poems on brown parcel tags
We suspend our books, our origami egrets, our passport photographs
Make table arrangements with your collection of corals & ferns
It keeps its record of us as we grow
Ours are the eggs in this cedar root basket

The Closing of the Exhibit

There are no answers for my mother & I
About the one her parents lost before
About the birth under anaesthesia
Or the decision not to behold the body
Nor the colour of the nursery
They shut the door on for six hopeless weeks

You wish it wasn't running down the stairs
Of our family,
Knocking on nursery room doors
We open ours again, step inside
Touch the curled up fur of the teddy in the crib
Hold each other, mouths wallpapered shut

The clothes fold back into boxes
We are loathe to open, loathe to close
But the museum hours lengthen
The exhibits dusted, carefully removed
Banners taken down
"Next time," says the Archivist

"Next time."

Emu, Petrified

Fossils & frail shells
The pregnant visitor rubs her belly
I trace my fingers over the glass

Somewhere in this building
Is a whole room full of eggs
Fossils & frail shells

Classes sweep through exhibits
Splitting, dividing, returning in rivers
The pregnant visitor rubs her belly

I hover over the ancient nest petrified
As time ticked past the birthing
I trace my fingers over the glass.

Closet Museum

At the entrance; my virginity, a vast crystal creature you half-recognise, wings splayed, white. Hanging just out of reach, its day seen, its sun set.
Beneath, an alabaster woman stands on tiptoes, cradled between her breasts a single pearl, wrapped in scarlet silk. You cannot read the sculptor's name. There are no signs. No timeline, no cretaceous period, but the exhibits close at midnight, Anno Domini.
The jewellery exhibit is modest but elegant & leads directly to the museum's "Boxed Items."
Between 11pm & 2am we host object handling sessions; a unique opportunity to explore the museum's private collection of artefacts; hats, mittens, socks & vests, journals, blankets, matching shirts, things worn once or not at all.
If you take a left & travel clockwise through "Coats & Shoes", you can examine almost the full spectrum of womanhood; browse examples of early Air Tones, Ballet Pumps, Blocks, Boots, Court Shoes, Canvas, Docs, Gladiators, Kittens, Mules, Platforms, Stilettoes & Wedges.
If you get up close you can hear the crippling.
A popular exhibit is the crying fountain at the north end of the museum. Throw in no pennies; they will only be spat back out at you. Though a dark space, this exhibit possesses a unique acoustic quality; stifling silence.
Make sure to visit the gallery in the east wing. The portraits are largely unfinished, but each is accompanied by a tremendous list of facts unknown until after the subject had departed.
If you purchased the tour on audiotape there are additional tracks which fantasise what could have become of each figure.
The gift shop is located on the other side of the "Blue Zone". For this last exhibit you must give a token. Once inside, stare up at the ceiling aimlessly,
feel small.

Museum of Flat-pack Furniture

Here are the 48 allen keys you swore you lost
Between the boxes & cracks of the floorboards
The pencil you put behind your ear to look more 'carpenterly'
You didn't use it once
Nothing trains a man to be a father like the flat-pack
It struggles & wails at you from the floor
You put everything on backwards
The pictures in the manual pulling at your patience
Here is the mug which spilt its steaming contents over them
& the three tea towels used to mop
Your brow, Doctor, inserting screw 123775 (1 of 4)
Into nut 100514 (1 of 3) with surgical precision
As though building it perfectly might protect it this time
As though it might do a better job than I have
Here are the photos I said I deleted
Propped against the second mug of coffee & the coaster
I yelled at you to use on the changing table
Last time you didn't build it, you put it off & we fought
You think that was bad luck
So this time the room is custard & the linen is cream
& when it's finished we lay on the rug stroking each other's faces
Like two kids painting a picket fence.

The Humours, the Lancet & the Leeches

The Tudor surgeon courts me in the hallway
His instruments sharp & twisting
It is the knees that go first when I feel it
The leeches moving down my thigh
Fingers scratch across the section label
'Spring was considered the time for bloodletting'
My own pale face in the glass tells me
You know this dance, this wicked practice
The imbalanced humours & the Doppler-handed Doctor
Shaking his head
We pull out of the office car park
& wait for the lights at the hospital
Your thumbs tap the steering wheel
Blood runs redder when you don't want it to
We hold our breath & count backwards from 10.

Museum of Broken Hands

Here, I must lay you down
With the others
Pale as plaster, heavy
We sing our lullabies
To Eros Sleeping
His quiet lips created
Still, unmoved for centuries
These children
Built wrong, built to last
In this alternate stream
I am the wrong kind of sculptor
My hands make no Cathedral
Glass arms offer up The Present
& your father takes his seat
As the Terme Boxer
Staring into heaven
His feet a melancholy sundial
You are timeless
& these, too, your brothers or sisters
Eternal fingers pointing inward
Over the face
Ageless

After Hours

Whale bones hang
Unmoving
Dressed in particles of dust
Ancient undisturbed
I climb to face it
In the gallery
& look it in the eye
Square
In the parchment hollow arch
Of its long bald socket
I lean close enough
To run fingers across the baleen
& like a harp
Hear its song
Ripple over ribs
So softly
I whisper
"Take me with you."

Natural History

Mr Finch is down the hall making his dead birds
I study the architecture blindly
Unseen, a small child mounts the back of a rhino

My coat is green as finches
I twirl so as to make the feathers dance
Mr Finch is down the hall making his dead birds

You reach out & recede in hesitance
Stammer over words which wanted to be an apology
I study the architecture blindly

We do this dance in silence down the aisles
Grafting ourselves eternally to our favourite exhibits
Unseen, a small child mounts the back of a rhino.

Higamus Hogamus

You make me a vase again
Like Rodin
Your hands worn soft with praying
Moulding round the smooth places
Touching eyes & face & hair
Languishing over the lips
Shaping back & breasts & belly
Kneading slow the points of weakness
Coaxing clay to firm, to harden, to hold
Hold what we put inside
After the fire
Hold now without breaking.

Christmas Display

For six weeks
We fold paper
Into animals
To decorate
The tree
We clink
Ornaments & glasses
Here we hope
Together
Beneath ladders & pine
I hang angels
In the wild cats exhibit
Mistletoe & snow
Amongst the native birds
You fill up the barrel
Of your chest & holler
Rejoice! Rejoice!
Seeking out my lips
Between the dance of
Robins & Starlings
We sing,
Ema-aaan-uel…
Mr Finch sews
Four calling birds
To send Maray
The door-cat
At the Serpukhov
For our international
Gift exchange
You turn them over
In your colossal palms
Echo the truth of his musing
"I suppose in every cushion
There *is* a tiny bird"
I rub against you & purr.

Extinction

There are many theories
Theories for the end

No explanation
Is concrete

- External Organisms
- Disease or parasites
- Caterpillars eating the food supply
- Disappearance of oily ferns
  Leading to death by constipation
- Over-kill by carnivores, perhaps
  Early mammals stealing eggs?
- Anatomic design
- Excessive body heat
- Cataracts, blindness induced
  by increases in ultra violet
- Diminishing brain size
  Death caused through stupidity
- Growth hormone malfunctions
- Slipped discs, hernias
- Progressive thinning of eggshells
- Stress induced conditions

We draw & fire
Arrows at the nearest culprit

The ifs, the must've-beens,
The hows, the howling whys

But we must remember:
Sometimes, things just end
You can do everything right,
& still

Life,
Might *not* find a way.

Heritage

We know little about this exhibit but scientists have come to
believe it had feathers
This is the beginning of the tour of my Grandmother's house
We already have an intuitive feel for this
In the dry store rooms of the museum they keep the hoard of
my Grandmother's prescriptions
One room for birds, another beetles, the next my
Grandmother's pharmacy
We tipped them all out on the bed once, counted the boxes of
paracetamol, 44
Buried the blankets in blister packets, careful not to drip
Bimatoprost over the French queen spread
The lipsticks next, the perfumes, pristine condition, six decks of
unused cards
There are great books laid open, filled with the lengthy rants of
my maternal Grandfather
Carefully placed beneath them are my Grandmother's two
word replies & a photograph.
They walk us through the Second World War with a quick step,
leaving several doors closed.
My Grandmother has black hair then. She cracks open one of
the displays & peers out at us.
I don't know if she scowls as we walk on, I expect instead that
she pretends not to have looked at all.
The recognition of what makes a genus or a family is partly a
matter of conscience
We wade through the drifts of shredded film piled on the
cutting room floor
What's left on the reels is all that I know
There are empty cases at the far end of the dim-lit hall
The Docent apologises
There are some creatures of which we only have the bones.

The Museum of Flightless Things

Bird collections operate much the same way as libraries do, with study skins arranged in cabinets full of drawers in their taxonomic order, only a fraction of the specimens we curate are here on display for you to see. All the rest are reserved for our resident scientists to analyse, & are occasionally loaned out for external studies.

Hidden

Birds tagged
Like celestial evacuees
Grounded here.
Silent babies & mothers,
Broken bodies
Empty nests

Quiet in quaking hands
Small,
Soft,
Graveless

Soft, small hands,

Quaking in quiet nests
Empty bodies
Broken mothers
& babies silent here,

Grounded,
Evacuees.
Celestial,
Like tagged birds, hidden.

The Smithsonian in Bed

On the Sundays we have left
We are sick with worry
Slick with fever sweat
You hold this body against the morning
Brush fingers through my hair
& vow to keep it all to yourself
Our wanderings roam
In ever constricting circles
Drawn down to a point

You open your mouth
Up to mine pressing
The Smithsonian into tree sap
Eyes & limbs contort
As windows arching
Cupping wings to the Earth
Sticky amber swallowing whole
With some kind of forgetting
Some kind of perfected time
Some kind of unreachable, lost

I drown in it
We climb the steps & point
With dizzy wonder at
The things we're not
Allowed to touch
& bend to make them
Soft in our hands
Shrill with excitement
Alive with the pleasure of it
Of hearts beating against the march
Our breaths hardening to marble
In the pits of our lungs burning

To escape with a cry
Your moan spills into silence
Echoes across the room
In the face of history

There are not many more places
We'll go together now
We pause in rooms to make love
Cradle each other naked as we reach the exit.

Two Cats from Onomichi

Akin to running up a hill
& sliding down again
Two wily cats to this day still
Launch bravely their campaign

To breach the gates, to enter in
To dodge the standing guard
To taste the arts which lay within
From which they have been barred

In this Museum hand in hand
Or rather paw in paw
Perhaps the pair might understand
Just what nine lives are for?

Day after day, week chasing week
For years & never tire
With never more than just a peek
At what they do desire

There is a moral to this tale
Two cats from Onomichi
Enduring in the place we fail
Oh how I wish they'd teach me

The Resurrection of Something Lost
(2019) Somewhere in Harvard

We regret to inform
You that this exhibit
Has been removed
Due to an unexpected
Case of spontaneous
Reanimation

Chinsekikan

'Jinmenseki'. A word we only learn later in life. Though of course it has been with us all along. Something you invented as a child. But never gave a name. Not knowing it had a name already. Like the cat which strayed. Stones with faces bluff & so often a child believes they are animate. Watching. The way a pair of disembodied fish eyes might stare up at you from the bottom of a bucket & your father, the scientist, might say 'How lovely' & ask you no more questions than that because he knew enough just by looking. But suddenly you've lost your taste for cold meats.

In this museum
Unseeing eyes belong to
The Jinmenseki.

Digital Art Museum

Then just like that
In one innocent motion
Light bleaches
Against the black
Mori becomes a forest
A rippling forest of lamps
Peach & pearl
Blossom & brunnera
Our bodies pulse
Touching
Seeking
Safe
Two loops
Woven
Yours & mine

A light
Now
From the other side
Of the room
Announces
That someone has joined us.

Gift Shop

I bought the moon
& rolled it from my palm
into my pocket.

Wondered how many times
great loved hands have waved
at me from space.

Wondered what I must have
swallowed in my sleep
to be seen from up there.

The cashier didn't seem
blinded by it, but I remember
that the moon is a mirror.

I take a last look at the stars
before I leave & mumble
Is it the sun then?

Am I some small component,
some happy fraction
of God's celestial periscope?

A for Mammals, B for Birds, C for Reptiles & so on

D is for Fish & Amphibians, for swimming, for this subaqueous phase, for the tickling joy you will find in the sandstone nodule shaped like a duck. Though you will not see it until we work down through the alphabet to M, for Rocks. E is for Molluscs, for muscles sewn tight in their places, staying right where they belong & not going anywhere. F is for Insects, for hungry caterpillars, for beautiful butterflies. G is for Arthropods, for Insy, for tuffets, for ladybirds safe in the rain. H is for the Soft Bodied Animals, for Tigger, for Roo, for the pinks & blues, for arms stretched out like stars. It is for mummies & daddies. For lambs & for teddies. For peach coloured sky & things being made new.

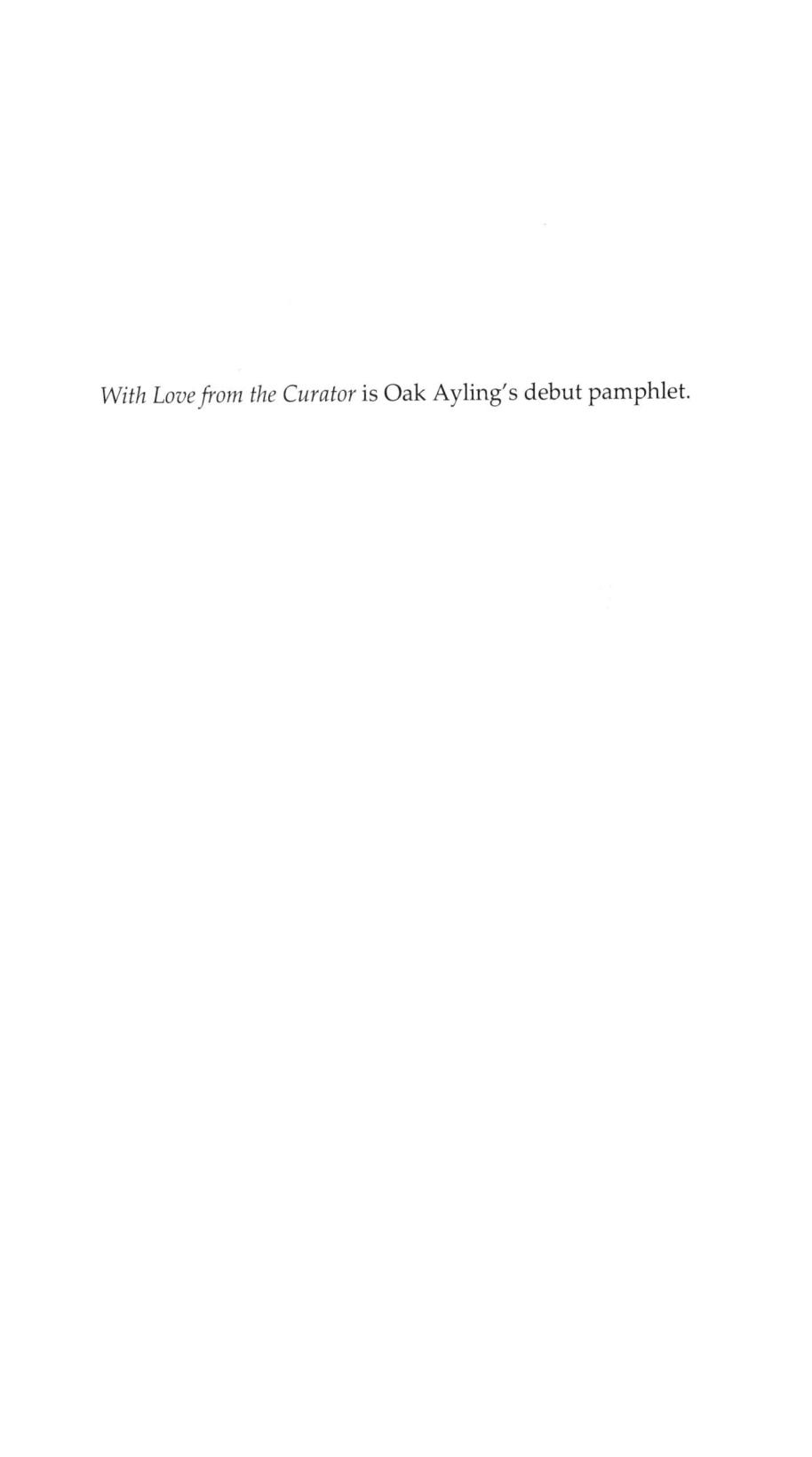

With Love from the Curator is Oak Ayling's debut pamphlet.

Indigo Dreams Publishing Ltd
24, Forest Houses
Cookworthy Moor
Halwill
Beaworthy
Devon
EX21 5UU
www.indigodreams.co.uk